To be a researcher, you must be willing to learn
new information and practice what you learn.
As you read this book, roll up your sleeves,
test your knowledge, and explore new possibilities!

MIX
Paper from
responsible sources
FSC® C118365

Copyright © 2022 Clavis Publishing Inc., New York

Originally published as *Knappe koppen. Alexander von Humboldt*
in Belgium and the Netherlands by Clavis Uitgeverij, 2021
English translation from the Dutch by Clavis Publishing Inc., New York

Visit us on the Web at www.clavis-publishing.com.

Great Minds. Alexander von Humboldt written by Peter Nys and illustrated by Conz
Assistant colorist: Amber R. Martin

ISBN 978-1-60537-743-8

This book was printed in November 2021 at Nikara, M. R. Štefánika 858/25, 963 01 Krupina, Slovakia.

First Edition
10 9 8 7 6 5 4 3 2 1

GREAT
MINDS

Alexander von Humboldt

Clavis
NEW YORK

Written by Peter Nys
Illustrated by Conz

lexander von Humboldt is a smart guy. But he's no bookworm! As a little boy, the German scientist prefers to roam the forests. Alexander loves anything found in nature, especially insects, plants, and stones. He learns a lot from his explorations. For instance, he learns that insects have six legs, stones have different colors, some plants like shade, and others don't. Alexander's pockets are always full of treasures, hence his nickname, *the little apothecary.*

Science begins with collection and classification. On a large piece of paper, draw a series of boxes. Write the following words above each column: insects, flowers, leaves, pebbles, shells, etc. Then go explore in your garden or neighborhood. Set each item you find in its own box. Questions to consider:

Does a spider belong with an ant?

Does an acorn belong with a pebble?

Why or why not?

Alexander is a homo universalis: someone who knows a lot about a wide variety of subjects. He was a mining engineer, explorer, climate scientist, geologist, inventor, surveyor, biologist, anthropologist, archeologist, laboratory technician, mathematician, tour guide, linguist, author, illustrator, consultant, and human rights activist. Do any of these professions interest you? If so, research what they entail and what training they require.

Miner's lamp

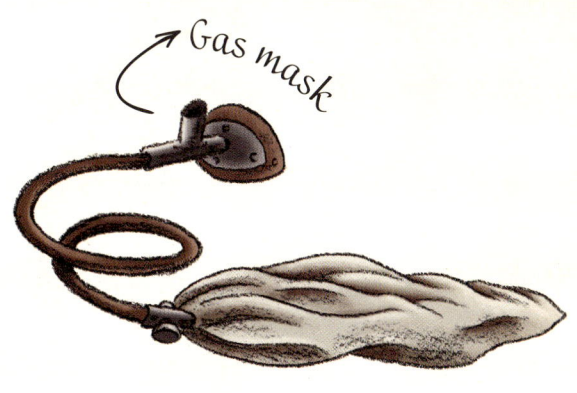
Gas mask

Later, Alexander becomes an inspector of mines. He's concerned about the safety of the miners and therefore invents a miner's lamp and a gas mask. In addition, the young scientist starts a school for miners. When they understand their environment better, they can work more safely. In his spare time, Alexander studies the fungi and mosses that grow in the faint light of the mines. He works on so many things at once that his colleagues joke he must have extra arms and legs.

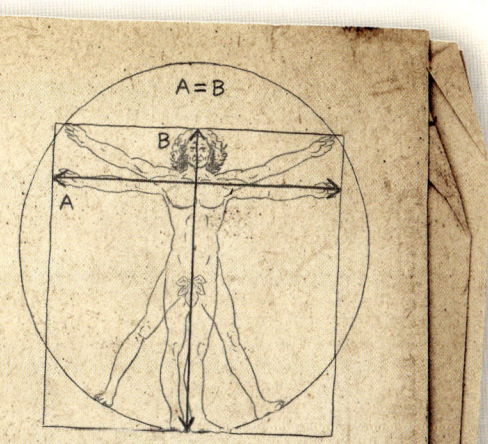
Wooden mouthpiece with air bellow

Try this: Stretch your arms horizontally and measure the distance from one fingertip to the other (A). This is equal to your height from head to toe (B).

A = B

In 1798, Alexander meets Aimé Bonpland, a young French botanist who also dreams of traveling far and wide. Alexander is very impressed when he learns that Aimé worked as a surgeon for the French navy. The young men become friends and embark on a journey of discovery together.

Napoleon Bonaparte, a French general, invades Egypt that same year. Alexander and Aimé want to follow him to the land of the pyramids and the Nile. They reach the French port of Marseille, but find no ship for Egypt. Instead they travel toward Spain. King Charles IV secures their passports for South America. Much of that continent hasn't yet been mapped. Alexander writes in his diary, "I feel in high spirits, just like you should when starting an important task."

In order to understand our past, we divide history into periods on a timeline. A timeline highlights important events in the order in which they occurred. For instance, the period from 1500 until 1800 is called the "modern age," which includes world-changing discoveries and inventions. Alexander and Aimé close this period with their expedition to South America. Then the "contemporary age" begins. List several world-changing discoveries and/or inventions from the modern or contemporary age. If you're unsure, conduct some research!

Try this: Make your own timeline and mark the most important moments in Alexander's life. There are several mentioned in this book.

1800

1900

1769
BIRTH
ALEXANDER

1798
NAPOLEON IN
EGYPT

Napoleon,
a French general

Pyramids
of Gizeh

Sphinx of Gizeh

Travel was drastically different in the 1800s. Research several differences from travel then and travel now. Would you consider traveling alone in the 1800s? Why or why not?

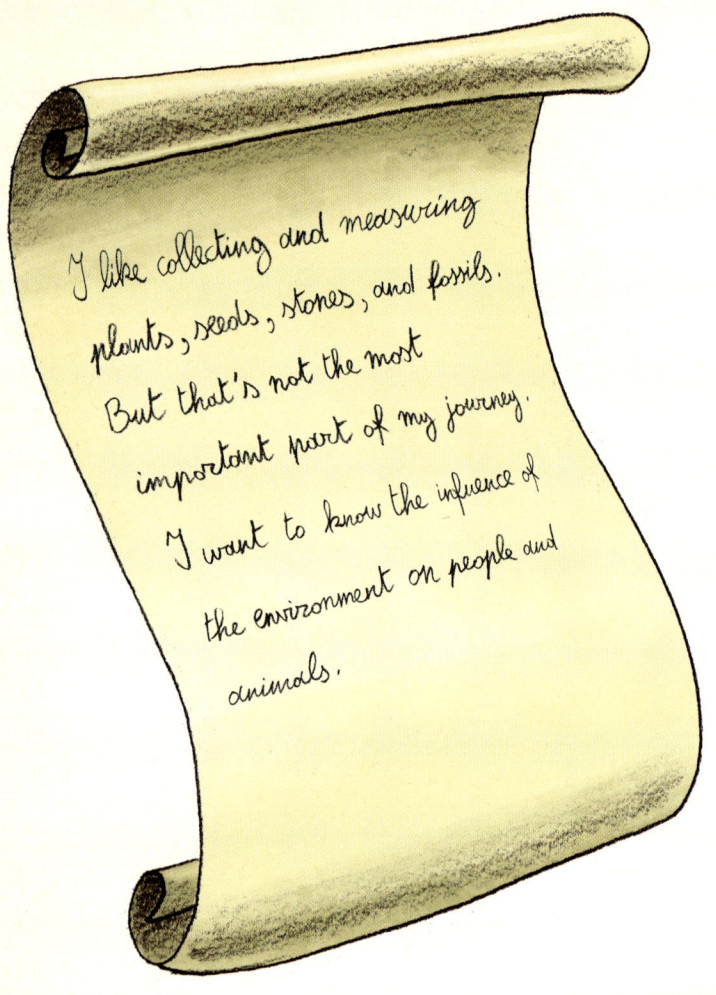

I like collecting and measuring plants, seeds, stones, and fossils. But that's not the most important part of my journey. I want to know the influence of the environment on people and animals.

Alexander is fond of measuring. He purchases an entire collection of instruments for his expedition: telescopes, microscopes, a thermometer, a clock, and a compass. Before he departs, he writes a letter. On June 5, 1799, Alexander and Aimé set off with all the instruments from La Coruña in Spain. Six weeks later, they arrive in Cumaná, Venezuela.

How do you measure the height of a tree? Fold a square piece of paper in half diagonally. This makes a triangle. With the tree in view, set a short side of the triangle parallel to the ground. Walk forward or backward until you see the tip of the tree at the top of the long side of the triangle. Draw a line in the ground. Now measure the distance from that line to the trunk of the tree. If you don't have a measuring stick, take large steps about the size of a meter (the distance between a doorknob and the ground). If you add your height to the measurement, you'll discover the height of the tree!

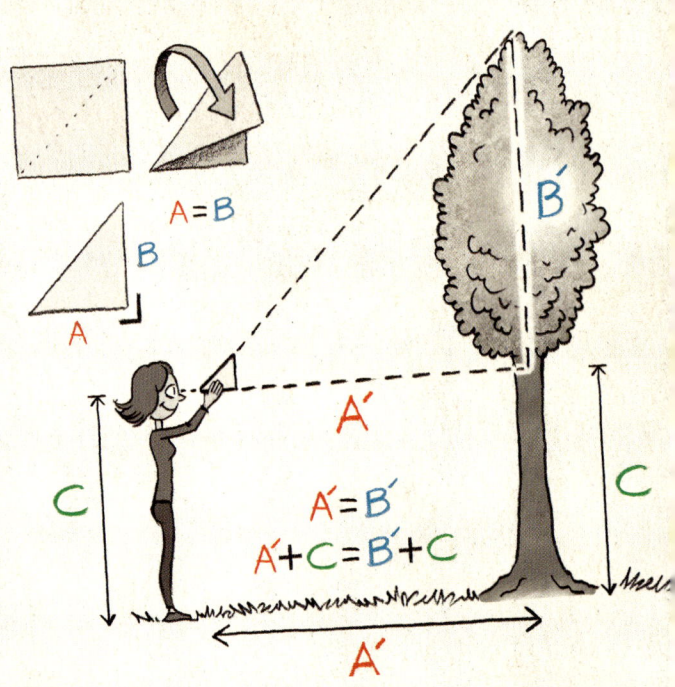

A = B

A' = B'

A' + C = B' + C

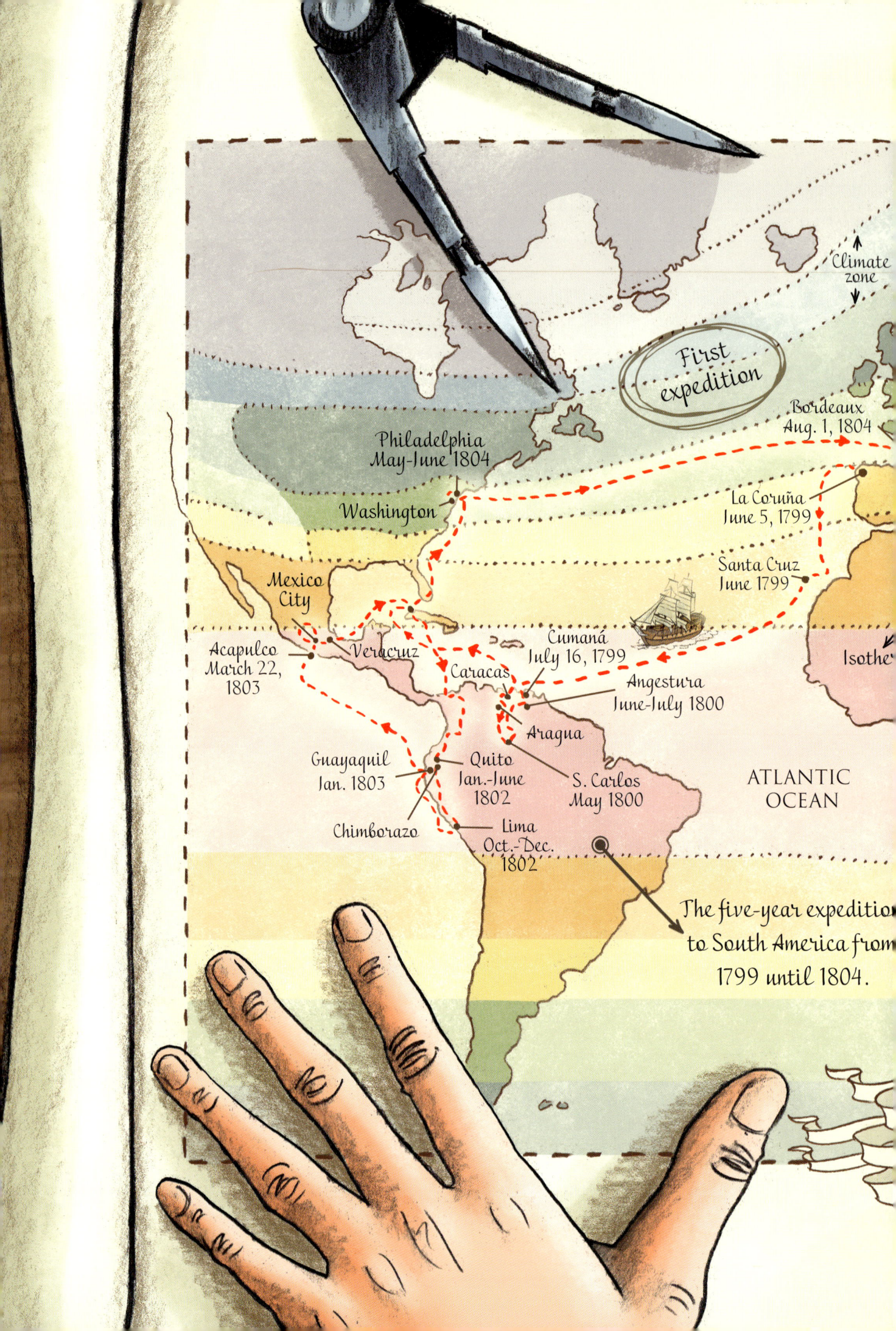

Climate zone

First expedition

Bordeaux
Aug. 1, 1804

Philadelphia
May-June 1804

La Coruña
June 5, 1799

Washington

Santa Cruz
June 1799

Mexico City

Cumaná
July 16, 1799

Isother

Acapulco
March 22, 1803

Veracruz

Caracas

Angestura
June-July 1800

Aragua

Guayaquil
Jan. 1803

Quito
Jan.-June 1802

S. Carlos
May 1800

ATLANTIC
OCEAN

Chimborazo

Lima
Oct.-Dec. 1802

The five-year expeditio
to South America from
1799 until 1804.

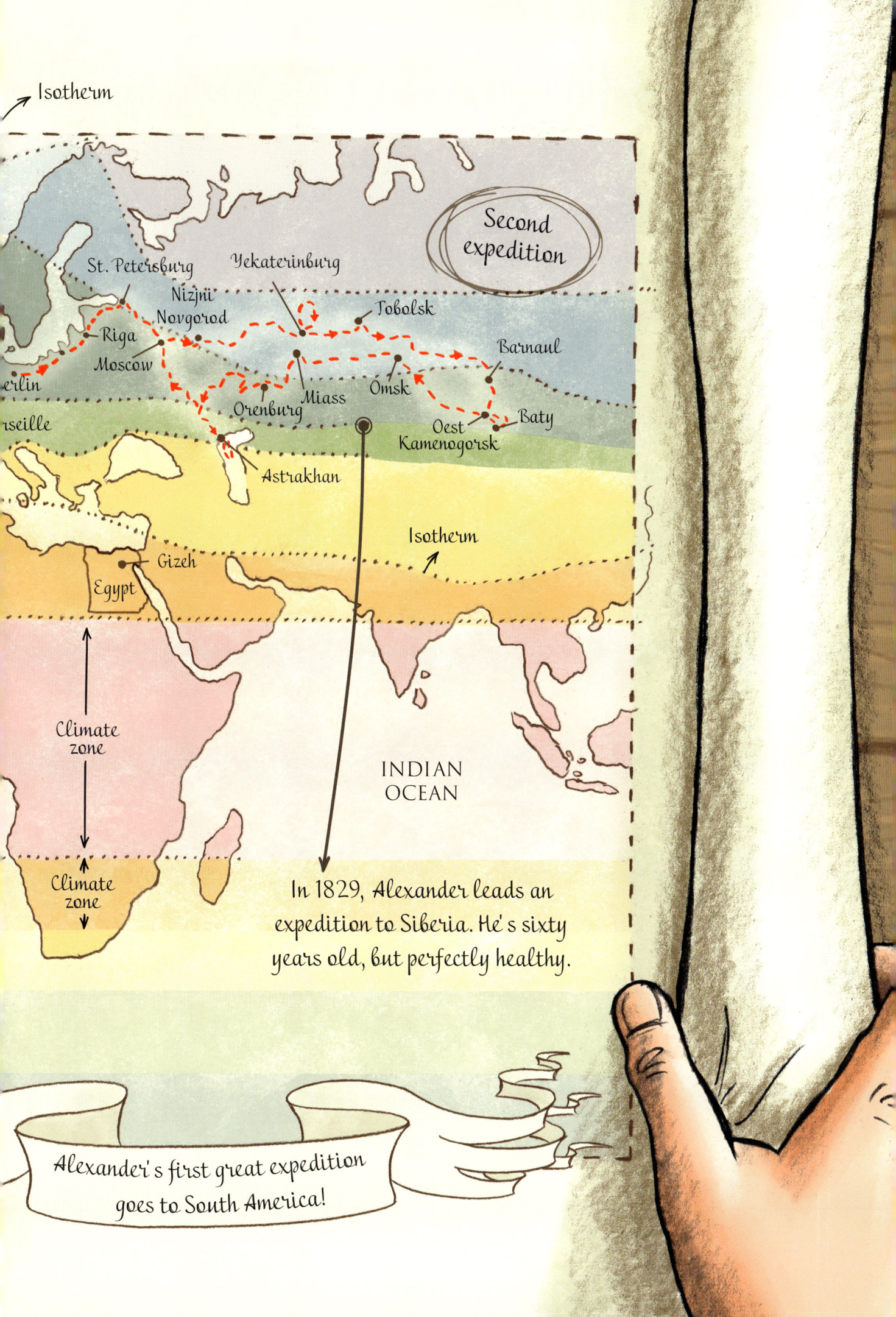

Isotherm

Second
expedition

St. Petersburg   Yekaterinburg

Nizjni
Novgorod   Tobolsk

Riga
Moscow   Barnaul

erlin   Omsk

rseille   Orenburg   Miass   Baty

Oest
Kamenogorsk

Astrakhan

Isotherm

Gizeh

Egypt

Climate
zone

INDIAN
OCEAN

Climate
zone

In 1829, Alexander leads an
expedition to Siberia. He's sixty
years old, but perfectly healthy.

Alexander's first great expedition
goes to South America!

On November 4, 1799, an earthquake rattles the adventurers in Cumaná. Houses collapse and people panic, but Alexander calmly climbs out of his hammock and sets up his instruments. He measures the time between shocks, and contemplates why the earth is trembling. Alexander discovers: the earth on which we stand can move, vibrate, and even crack!

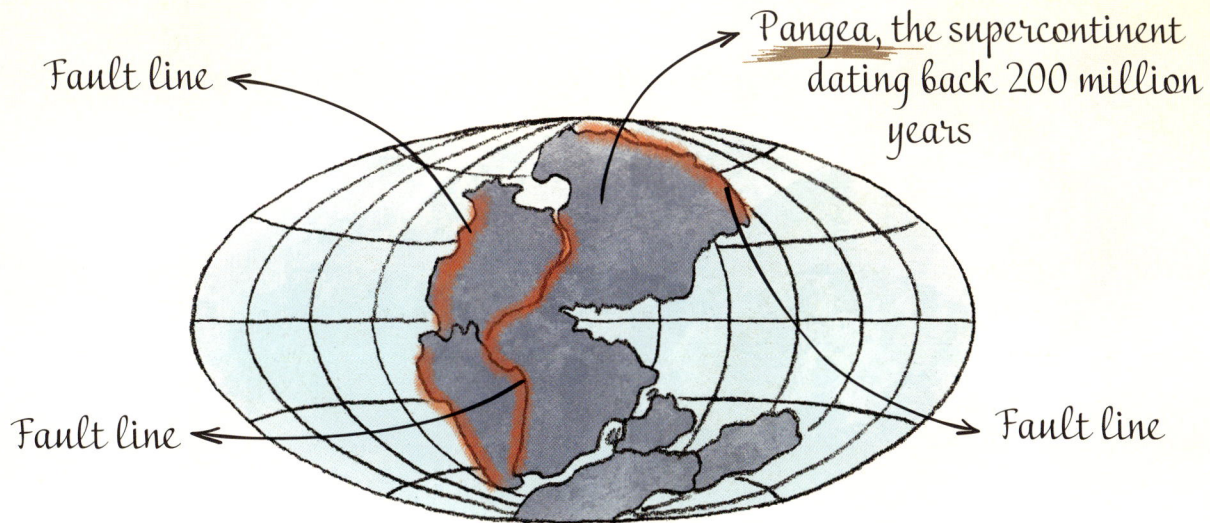

Pangea, the supercontinent dating back 200 million years

Fault line

Fault line

Fault line

In Alexander's time, most people believed that the earth is changeless. Today, we know that earthquakes occur when pieces of the earth's crust rub against or slide beneath each other. We call this plate tectonics. The rubbing and sliding happens very slowly, but occasionally causes violent earthquakes or volcanic eruptions, especially on fault lines.

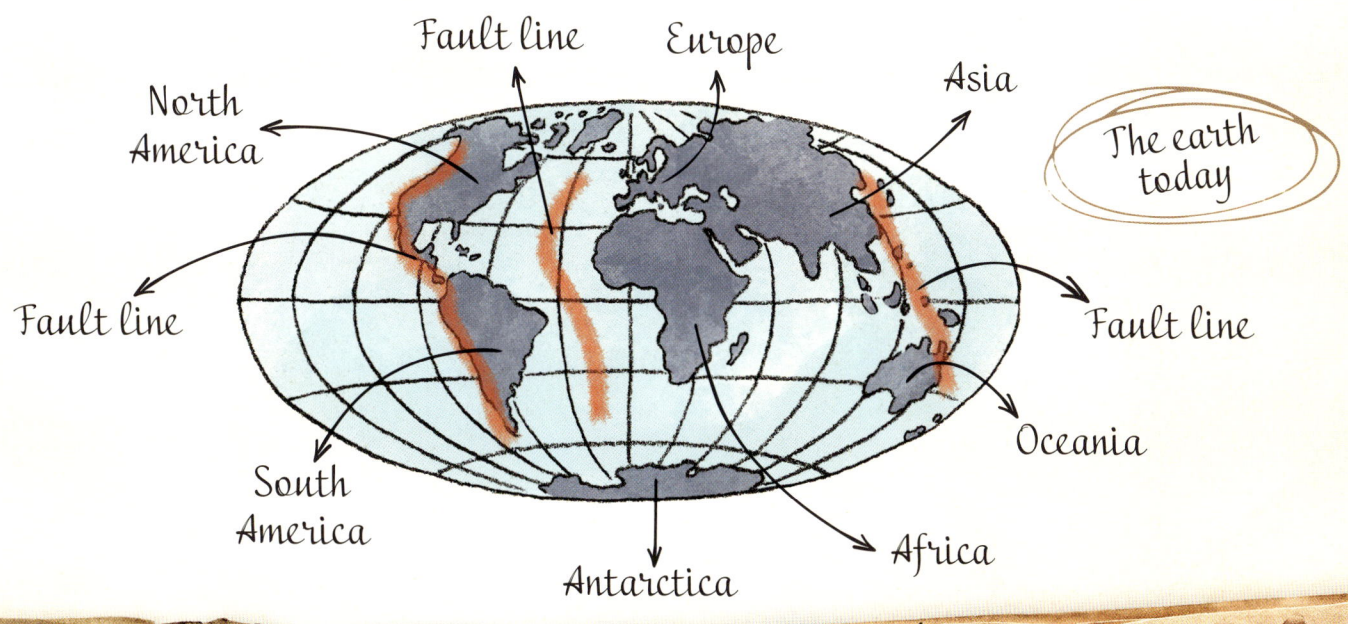

Fault line

Europe

Asia

North America

The earth today

Fault line

Fault line

South America

Oceania

Antarctica

Africa

The speed at which the plates move varies from 1 millimeter (.04 inch) to 2 centimeters (.8 inch) a year. That corresponds to the speed at which a fingernail grows.

Have you ever watched a cup of hot milk cool? A thin layer forms on its surface. Continental plates are similar, they're like thin, solidified crusts floating atop hot lava, deep in the earth. Their crust causes the plates to shift.

A few months later, Alexander and Aimé travel to the Orinoco, a large river in South America. In the Aragua Valley, they hear a peculiar story: <u>the water level</u> of Lake Valencia has been <u>dropping for years!</u> The locals think there's a hole in the bottom. Alexander doesn't believe it. He discovers the real cause: the felling of trees for agriculture. This causes the shrubbery to disappear, allowing the sun to evaporate the water from the soil. Not only is the earth changeable, but humans play a role in it!

In the eighteenth century, western people believe that God created the earth so perfectly that it can't change. Alexander is one of the first scientists to challenge this idea. He finds that the earth is constantly changing, often because of people. Can you think of any examples of the earth changing? How are people responsible for these changes?

What's the highest mountain in the world?
It just depends on how you look at it!
Consider these world records: Mount Everest
is 8.8 kilometers (5.5 miles) above sea level. Mauna Kea is
10 kilometers (6.2 miles) high from its base under water.
And the Chimborazo is 6,384.3 kilometers (3,967 miles)
from the center of the earth.

Chimborazo
6,384.3 km (3,967 mi)

8.8 km (5.5 mi)

Mount Everest

10 km (6.2 mi)

Mauna Kea

Alexander is not only a climate genius, but also a true adventurer! In June 1802, he and Aimé climb the Chimborazo, a high volcano near the equator.

When Alexander nearly reaches the top, a deep gorge blocks the way to the peak of the volcano. Alexander looks around. He's wearing ordinary clothes at more than 6,000 meters (19,685 feet), and it's freezing cold. He notices his surroundings: plants, animals, rocks, temperature, air pressure . . . everything is tied together like the threads in a giant cobweb.

All living things are made of carbon atoms. Plants, people, and animals must absorb carbon atoms to grow. The carbon atoms are like Legos with which the body is built. Animals and people absorb carbon atoms through food, while plants receive them from the air. When plants, animals, or people die, their carbon atoms are reabsorbed by the earth. It's a cycle.

Carbon

Carbon
Water

Water

Can you guess why the leaves of trees in temperate regions have a large surface area, and the leaves of trees in cold regions tend to be needle-shaped? Begin by investigating how leaves play a supportive role. Also consider the vulnerability of trees in the winter.

Back at the foot of the mountain, Alexander creates a beautiful drawing of the mighty Chimborazo. He draws the tropical forest with layers of deciduous trees and ferny shrubbery ascending to the snowy peaks. His head spins: every climatic zone can be found on this one mountain. In this moment, Alexander becomes the "inventor" of climate. Alexander's drawing, *Naturgemälde*, is printed and made available for purchase. It sells thousands of copies!

Alexander is also the inventor of tracking temperatures on a map. We call these lines isotherms. The area between two lines is a climate zone. You can find them on the world map in this book. Scientists still use them today for weather reports. Use the illustration on the left to find the climate zones on the flanks of the Chimborazo. Notice how the peak on a mountain in the warm south has the same climate as the northern countries. Both locations have similar plants!

Try this: Find a plant or flower and draw it. Is it easy or difficult? Why or why not?

Alexander is ahead of his time. He's the first climate activist! Are you aware of any climate activists today? How can you play an active role in your environment?

Alexander returns to Europe after a detour through Mexico and the United States. While in the United States, he's invited to visit the White House! Later he travels to Siberia, where he experiences the impact of deforestation and large-scale irrigation on the climate. Alexander warns of factory pollution . . . advice issued more than two hundred years ago!

The atmosphere, a gas shell around the globe, acts like a warm blanket. The more carbon that enters the air from burning oil or gas, the thicker that blanket becomes. Scientists agree that the average world temperature mustn't rise more than 2 degrees Celsius (35.6 degrees Fahrenheit) by the year 2050. To achieve this, we must start living smarter with eco-friendly cars, fewer planes, efficient heating systems, and less consumption of animal meat. If everyone does their part, we will succeed!

Alexander von Humboldt, father of the climate movement

In 1834, Alexander begins writing a book in which he outlines the entire cosmos. It amounts to five volumes of content! Alexander becomes world famous.

Humboldt lily

Humboldt penguin

Many animals, plants, places, and institutes are named after Alexander von Humboldt. His books on the cosmos are the only books Charles Darwin takes with him on his worldwide voyage on his ship, the Beagle.